*"Adam Green is to Financial Free[dom]* [what] *taxi industry... Disruptive, Inven*[tive,] *Visionary. Most 25 year olds are still trying to figure out how to get a job while Adam is figuring out the 'payoff' on his home loan so he can stroke a check and be debt free. He has figured out the wealth building model of Network Marketing and in this book he shows you how you can do it too. Adam is the future of the network marketing profession. He will create hundreds of millionaires... if not thousands. Listen to him. Study him. Follow him. Duplicate him and the world will be your playground."*

—Richard Bliss Brooke (SuperMLMMan)
Author, *"The Four Year Career"* and
*"Mach II: The Art of Vision and Self Motivation"*

*"Adam Green has figured out in his first 25 years what most people spend their entire life seeking and never find. He has discovered how to win at business and in life. This book will open your eyes on an alternate path to the life of your dreams."*

—Dr. Dave Braun and Dr. Troy Amdahl
Co-Authors, *"Oola: Find Balance in an Unbalanced World"*

*"Adam Green is the real deal. Successful people in business are everywhere. But Adam is significant because he is creating successors, by helping others to achieve great heights in his footsteps. His heart and desire are enormous, and he is worth modelling."*

—Brian Carruthers
Author, *"Building an Empire"* and *"Making My First 10 Million"*

*"Youth. It can work for you ... or against you. Adam makes youth work for him. He sets the example that we don't have to wait until we are old to figure out that having a job simply interferes with our week. Why not design the life you want earlier rather than later?"*

—Tom "Big Al" Schreiter
43 Year Network Marketing Veteran, Author of 15 Books
www.BigAlBooks.com

*"Adam Green is a servant leader. From the knowledge he shares with his team--to the resources and time he and his wife Vanessa share with those in need. He is living a life of significance, and achieving what most twice his age still dream of doing."*

—Sarah Robbins, Network Marketing Leader
Author: *"Rock Your Network Marketing Business"*

*"When I was Adam's age I sat in a cubicle as a draftsman for the State of Arizona. Sitting across from me was an old guy named Elvio that had been working out of the same cubicle for 25 years. I remember having the experience of feeling imprisoned in a job that I despised! I needed to "break out"! I didn't want to end up like Elvio! This was a defining moment in my life. As I read Adam's book, I was taken back to the formative years in my networking career. I began to reflect on what a profound transformation Adam's book will have on young networkers around the globe."*

—Jordan Adler, Network Marketing Millionaire,
Author: *"Beach Money"*

# JAILBREAK YOUR 9-5
## & Escape to Financial Freedom

# ADAM GREEN

ISBN 978-0-9936797-0-4

Printed in Canada

First Edition

# TABLE OF CONTENTS

# FOREWORD

One of the best things about being in the People Business is that you get to meet and learn the stories of so many characters. We are all so different, yet at our core so much alike. The People Business I have been in since 1977 is Direct Selling or, more specifically, Network Marketing. 475,000 people a week join our profession in any one of 1,000 different companies, all with a little or large dream of earning more money.

Sadly, most never realize their dream. Not because they couldn't, not because the business model is flawed (it is not perfect but it does work in a very powerful way), and not because they didn't want it badly enough. Most never realize their dream because they just did not do the things they were coached or taught to do. They subscribed to the philosophies of Try, Maybe, Hope and Getting Ready instead of Just Do It or, as I like to say, Just Do It Anyway.

Every once in a while out of the tens of thousands of people I have met, I meet a leader. Someone with a big dream … a dream bigger than all their excuses and circumstances. And someone with that special something … that special voice in their heart that tells them every day, Just Do It Anyway. And they follow that voice down a yellow brick road to freedom and abundance.

Adam Green is one of those leaders.

I first met Adam in Coeur d'Alene, Idaho. He asked me for an hour of my time to guide him. He drove 18 hours round trip for that one hour. We made it two. He was already successful. He just wanted it all to really count for something. He wanted to do it right, to inspire people to do it right and to build something extraordinary. And he did. And he is not even remotely finished. In fact, he is just getting started.

I am glad I am still young enough to see the impact on millions of people that Adam Green will have ... anyone with a dream and the courage to pursue it. This is his first book. Just enough of his story to pique your interest. He is 25 years old, debt and financially free, and all done in less than four years. I can only imagine what books he will write in the next 40 years.

Adam Green is the future of Ethical Network Marketing. He can and will show you how to build your own freedom and do it in a way that honors and contributes to others. I am honored to call him my friend and one of my few Inspirations.

Rock on, Adam.

—Richard Bliss Brooke
Author, *"The Four Year Career"*
and *"Mach II: The Art of Vision and Self Motivation"*

# WHY YOU SHOULD READ
# THIS BOOK

I don't believe in coincidences. I know you are reading this book for a reason, and that it has come into your life at the perfect time. We all have 24 hours in a day, but we choose to spend them differently, and thus get different results. I've spent my time in a way that, in the past four years, I have been able to go from college graduate to personal trainer to millionaire. So I guess you could say I have spent my 24 hours differently.

I never pictured myself as an author growing up, but then again I never pictured myself being debt free, owning my own home (and life), and having it all completely financed through passive income. My goal in writing this book is to provide a beacon of hope and inspiration to a generation plagued by student loans, buried in debt, and living paycheck to paycheck. I have high hopes that stories like mine can inspire others to change the way they look at the world, and create a cascade of change and hope in a world that truly needs it.

If you are holding this book, my assumption is you are looking to brighten your financial future. You have bigger dreams than your current income provides, and are looking for answers on how to live a life filled with true purpose. Or, maybe someone has passed this book along to you in hopes of inspiring and motivating you. However you acquired this book, I am glad you have it.

The question I urge you to ask yourself is: How would it change your life if, after working differently for the next four to five years, you were close to becoming a multimillionaire, you had total financial freedom, and your income was on track to increase more than 200 percent a year, and it all was not produced by a business that, in a sense, owned you? What if you weren't strapped down to work countless hours a day, but you had total freedom? What if you were able to enjoy freedom of movement, living anywhere in the world you wanted to live, without disrupting your income model?

I have laid out my story in this book. It is a story of how I escaped the traditional life sentence of working away the best years of my life, and created financial freedom for myself and a life filled with purpose. Whether you have stumbled upon this book yourself or someone has invested in your future by giving it to you, I implore you to take the time to read it. The Number One thing I hear from others when I am traveling the world sharing my story is, "I wish my spouse/child/friend could have been here to hear your story." I have had the privilege of traveling to more than 30 countries before the age of 25 in order to share how I have been able to create not only financial freedom, but time freedom, in a way you were likely never taught about in school.

Not only have I accomplished this legally, but I have also been able to coach and inspire countless others to achieve this same feat. My wish for you is that you will be open minded in reading this book. One of the most expensive things you can own is a closed mind.

I will open up my heart in the pages you have in front of you. I encourage you to open your mind as you open this book. You just might open up a door to opportunity and change that will allow you to escape your 25 to Life.

# CHAPTER
# ONE

*Escaping My Life Sentence*

Living out a life sentence was not what I was cut out for. Being rudely awakened by the blaring sound of my alarm clock with no snooze button in sight, slipping my keys into the ignition of my '99 Civic on cold frosty mornings and wishing I was back in the warmth of my bed, thinking of doing this day in and day out and leaving my family at home while I was at the office, looking at their pictures instead of spending time with them ... Was this to be my lot in life?

The endless hours stuck in traffic, daydreaming of everything I wished I was doing, was getting harder every day. I felt suffocated, working 40-plus hours a week and living for the weekend, when I could finally feel freedom, even if for only two days. I was trapped in my own little prison, with no way to break out … or so it seemed.

You see, this life sentence was a self-imposed one, one I had actually signed up for and paid for. I bought and locked myself into a paradigm that seemed inevitable, inescapable, and just the way things were supposed to be done. I was living the only way I knew was possible, doing what I was told, and following the beaten path.

"Twenty-five to Life" is the terminology used to refer to prison sentences for criminals. Many governments believe the worst sentence for a criminal is to spend the rest of his or her life behind bars.

However, many more people in the world are living out their own prison sentences, just not behind bars. They serve their sentences in cubicles, behind desks, and in the trenches of mediocrity, constantly grinding day in and day out, struggling to keep themselves afloat. These prisoners are not wearing black-and-white striped jumpsuits, but instead are adorned with suits, ties, smocks, and work uniforms. Ball and chains are replaced with mountains of debt we carry on our shoulders wherever we go, a heavy reminder of the reason we trade the best 40-plus years of our life: To make a living with the hopes of retiring and enjoying our "golden years."

This was the sentence I had purchased for myself. I purchased it by investing tens of thousands of dollars into a post-secondary education, under the belief that good grades and an expensive degree would position me to get a job that could hopefully provide for me and my family for the next 40-plus years of my life. This was the paradigm I was raised in, trained in, and preened for since the age of five, much like the rest of the modern-day first world. Humans are creatures of habit. We are formed based on our environment, our experiences, and the behavior that is modeled to us. Almost all of us spend 12-plus years, from age five onward, being preened in the school system. We are taught what we are supposed to learn according to an established curriculum. We try to fit into cookie cutter molds set out for us to get a "passing grade."

On average, students receive more than 7,500 hours of instruction in their primary and lower secondary education, with students in some countries receiving more than 10,000 hours of educational time. Recent research has found that the total time in school matters less than how the time is spent, on which subjects, and the strength of the curriculum.[1] Put simply, more time in class does not always lead to improved learning outcomes for students in core subjects. We are, in essence, spending more time studying the wrong subjects, and not enough time studying the subjects we should be learning.

The behavior modeled to most of us by our parents, teachers, and other adults--that of getting good grades, a great education, and then finding a good job until retirement--comes with good intentions, I am sure. But it would be ignorant to think that this is the only way to succeed/live life. Often, when we challenge the system and move in a different direction from the masses, we are met with criticism for our different thoughts and actions, much of it from close friends and family who are sincerely worried about our "new direction." But these people can be sincerely wrong.

Now, given the option of having higher education or no education, becoming educated still has its value, but maybe not for the reasons we invest in it. As a model, higher education is crippling more students with massive debt loads they are not equipped to deal with. Total student loan debt in the United States surpassed $1 trillion in 2011,

---

1        www.oecd.org/edu/skills-beyond-school/EDIF%202014--N22%20(eng).pdf

which is more than the nation's entire credit card debt. Not even declaring bankruptcy can free you from this burden. "Bankruptcy is supposed to be the last chance for the honest but unfortunate debtor," according to the Canadian Federation of Students. "Yet, since 1998, students who were forced to borrow to finance post-secondary education have been subjected to a law prohibiting bankruptcy on student loans for many years after graduation. In effect, students with debt have been criminalized and are faced with the same type of penalty as those convicted of fraud."[2]

In Canada, recent statistics show that the average graduate's debt load takes, on average, 14 years to pay off.[3]

I was one of the "lucky" ones, having invested only two years of my life and approximately $60,000 into my post secondary (tuition, books, living expenses, lost wages, etc.). That was nearly all of my life savings, which I had hustled for and worked for since I was 14 years old. This $60,000 piece of paper gave me the opportunity to get a job as a personal trainer, where I could work 40-50 hours a week, split shifts, and hopefully earn $30,000 a year and get two weeks of vacation (which in today's world ends up being a staycation for most people). The job market today is one in which an employer pays you just enough to keep you from quitting, and you work hard enough to keep them from firing you, with no real opportunity for the average person to break out of this life sentence. This was the situation I found myself in as a college graduate five years ago. I was not your average college graduate, since I graduated without any student

---

2        http://cfs.bc.ca/section/48
3        http://business.financialpost.com/2012/09/04/student-debt-aver-age-payback-takes-14-years/

loans. But I was one of the many individuals destined to be trapped in this prison sentence not just for 25 years, but for at least 40, with no opportunity to get out early for good behavior.

However, I discovered a way to escape not through good behavior, but different behavior. Einstein stated so brilliantly, "Insanity is doing the same thing over and over again, and expecting a different result." I realized I was insane if I followed the path laid out in front of me for the next 40 years, and somehow expected a different result than the millions who had also followed the same route. In order to reach a different destination, I needed to have a different path and different behaviors. The traditional Plan A was flawed ... I needed a Plan B. I discovered by shifting my mindset, my actions, and the model upon which I built my life, I could break out and do something great with my life and experience true freedom.

# CHAPTER
# TWO

*25 to Life: A Different Kind of Life Sentence*

Today, at just 25 years old, I have created a new meaning for 25 to Life. Instead of a life sentence in the work force, I escaped. I challenged the system, the way things were "supposed to be," and in a short four to five years broke out from my personal life sentence as an employee.

Now, 25 to Life is a life based on complete financial freedom at the age of 25, having my entire life ahead of me to live life to the fullest, while helping others escape their own life sentence. I was able to achieve this through different actions, which produced different results.

These different actions have led me to where I am today, 25 years old, earning a seven figure annual income. On August 14th, 2014, I wrote a check for the remaining balance of my mortgage, officially becoming debt free. I have 35,000 business partners in 30 countries from which I earn royalties every month. My income has been increasing more than 200 percent annually for the past three years, with a very high probability of that continuing every year.

Is the life-paradigm of achieving good grades in high school, going to a decent college, and getting a good job ever going to provide that kind of outcome for you?

Here is the truth about today's paradigm: You may not end up working for some factory for 40 years like in past generations, but your career will still be based on getting a good job and staying there until you find a better job. You will face a constant cycle of job after job after job, spending 90 percent of your waking hours worrying about how to pay the bills, how to get ahead, how to invest, how to get a better job or a pay raise, how to get more recognition and a better standing at work, how to spin all the plates of life without them crashing down around you. Unfortunately, what happens for most people is they never get far enough ahead to get out of the rat race. They end up being 60, 70, 80 years old, and they are still oppressed by the weight of the system. They are a victim of it as opposed to being on top of it.

The question I urge you to ask yourself is: How would it change your life if, after working differently for the next four to five years, you were close to becoming a multimillionaire, you had total financial freedom, and your income was on track to increase more than 200 percent a year, and it all was not produced by a business that, in a sense, owned you? What if you weren't strapped down to work countless hours a day, but you had total freedom? What if you were able to enjoy freedom of movement, living anywhere in the world you wanted to live, without disrupting your income model? AND consider that you wouldn't even need to keep driving that income model to benefit from it, you could actually do anything you wanted to do for a living or for fun. Where would you live? What would your family be like? What church would you serve? What would you create? What kind of service would you provide the world? What kind of contribution would you make? What book would you publish? What would you invent? What songs or poetry would you write? What villages would you build? Now that sounds like the kind of life sentence I would want to serve.

No matter where you are in your life, it is not too late to course correct to attain different results than what you are currently headed for. And the perfect time to make the shift is today.

# CHAPTER
# THREE

*Making the Shift*

The shift I am proposing is the shift to being financially free and doing it in four years as opposed to grinding away with the strategy of hope for 40 years, only to be disappointed at the 40-year mark. Moving faster in the wrong direction doesn't get you closer to your dreams any quicker. If we are to achieve different results, we need to change the direction in which we are moving, and the sooner the better. As the late entrepreneur and author Jim Rohn once said, "For things to change, we have to change. For things to get better, we have to get better."

For those who remain in the workforce as an employee, with that job being their only means of income, my prediction as to where they will most likely be at the end of the next four years is: exactly where they are now! Even given a small annual raise (and recent statistics show the majority of employers–62 percent—plan to keep salaries the same as the previous year) will translate into a slight decline in income, given inflation.[*4]

---

4    www.ceri.msu.edu/wp-content/uploads/2014/10/CERI-press-release-10-27-14-starting-salaries-FINAL1.pdf

I have discovered through experience that the most logical starting point for achieving something new and uncharted is by following the example of someone who has achieved the results you are looking for. My advice is to choose someone, follow their model, and get their results.

I sought out people who had broken free of debt, escaped from their jobs, and established a life built on financial and time freedom. Every day I would strive to associate with people who were getting the results in life I desired, and to limit my exposure to those who had results I wanted to avoid. If you are looking to escape to the life of your dreams, you need to employ the Law of Association. Jim Rohn said it best: "You become the average of the five people you spend the most time with." One of the first shifts in breaking free was analyzing who I was spending my time with and how that would affect my future. If you hang around five people who are not content with their life plan (or don't have one), you have a tough journey ahead of you as you work on your own dreams! As a very brief exercise, write down the five people you associate with the most in your life. Check your cell phone statement, and see who you call/text the most in your life, then look at all areas of their life and how they might reflect on your own life. This simple exercise/idea shifted the future of my own life, as I began to change who I primarily associated with. I focused on surrounding myself with individuals who had lives filled with positivity, healthy finances, rich relationships, and fulfillment. You would be wise to associate with people who have achieved what you want to achieve, and place value where you see value.

In order to escape, we need to shift away from the employee mindset we were raised with and find a model that supports our dreams and goals for freedom. We need to realize that we have our priorities backwards in our current model of employment, where the only way we earn an income is by trading time for dollars. This model is based 100 percent on your own efforts, and if you don't work you don't get paid. What happens if your health takes a turn for the worse, and you can't work for a while? How will you support your family's essential needs, not to mention the dreams of those you love, if the only way you can earn money is by exchanging time for it? As a culture, we treat money like it is finite, spending all the money we have (and more, by increasing our debt), and our time like it is infinite, living for "someday dreams" with no real time frame for achieving all we would love to in life. Today, your mindset needs to shift, and realize that time is the ONLY limited commodity, something that once you spend you can never get back. Since time is our true limited and valuable commodity, this is the resource we need to guard closely and spend wisely. We need to realize that wasting our time is much worse than wasting our money. For most people, that is a dramatic shift in their thinking.

One of the most expensive things you can have is a closed mind. Sometimes, all it takes is a few simple words to give you a proper wake up call. For me, the realization that time is the only limited commodity is what shifted the direction of my life. I knew I had to make a shift and find ways to create time freedom, which would then lead to financial freedom.

Most people have bought into what has been coined the 40/40/40 plan. That is, to work for 40 hours a week, for 40 years, and retire on 40 percent of their income. This seems normal to most people, as it is how we are brought up as a society. When everyone around you is on the same path, you have no reason to believe there is a better way. For most people, this is Plan A.

| PLAN A | TRADITIONAL EMPLOYMENT |
|---|---|
| 40 Hours a Week | |
| 50 Weeks a Year | |
| 40 Years | |
| 80,000 hours of cumulative work | |

Working 40 hours a week, 50 weeks a year, for 40 years equals a total of 80,000 hours of working to reach the end goal of "retirement" and hopefully having enough passive income at the age of 65 to not have to work for the remainder of your days. With this model, you have a boss, a tightly managed schedule, no residual income developed, and limited growth opportunity. This model might earn you a living, but never a fortune or time freedom. Beyond the financial aspect of employment, this plan is filled with people who are unsatisfied and unhappy with their work. Dissatisfied employees outnumber happy employees 2:1, with only 13 percent of people who feel actively engaged in their position.[5] Not only are we all searching for ways to earn more money, but we are searching for ways to contribute, engage, and have meaningful existence in a field we are passionate about.

Job security in this paradigm—Plan A—is not what it used to be. With the average person staying at their job for only 4.1 years, you are likely to have 7 to 10 jobs in your

---

5        www.forbes.com/sites/susanadams/2013/10/10/unhappy-employees-outnumber-happy-ones-by-two-to-one-worldwide/

lifetime. Most companies are looking out for their bottom line and for ways to maximize their profits, often cutting expenses and fat around the edges, which often ends up being employees. In 2015, Burger King acquired the Canadian coffee tycoon Tim Hortons in a $11 billion deal, which led to corporate downsizing inside the Tim Hortons franchise. The result: downsizing close to 20 percent of the staff, including pregnant women and staff who had been with the chain for 30 years.[6] With job security being virtually nonexistent, we would be wise to have a financial plan that is not tied to our current job.

If this is our Plan A, then I think we would be wise to have a Plan B, a backup plan. The real way to earn an income without trading our most valuable commodity—time—is to develop residual or passive income. You need to have leverage.

I'm sure the biggest question at this point is, "How?" How do I make this shift? How do I create leverage? How is this even possible and why have I not been taught about this in school? That indeed is the million-dollar question, and the key to freedom. It is time for us to have a better escape plan.

---

6       www.cbc.ca/news/business/tim-hortons-layoffs-long-time-employees-escorted-out-the-door-1.2934853

# CHAPTER
# FOUR

*The Great Escape*

The key to my success when it comes to creating a life of financial freedom was discovering a unique business model that allowed me to have all the benefits of a business owner, without the usual costs of starting a business. There are many benefits to being a traditional business owner, but there are also some major drawbacks. Number One, for me, was the initial cost required to start a business. Also, with a traditional brick and mortar business, at the end of the day, you are often tied to a business that owns you more than you own it.

If I were to lay out all the benefits I would want in a business, it would look like:

- Unlimited earning potential
- Flexible (lifestyle friendly)
- Low start-up cost
- No education required (learn while you earn)
- Ability to empower others to succeed as well
- Tax advantages
- Residual
- Will-able

Initially, I thought this type of dream business didn't exist, was too good to be true. I couldn't have been more wrong. I discovered everything I was looking for when I stumbled upon the wealth building profession of network marketing.

This well-established business model has been effectively moving high quality products and services into the marketplace for more than 70 years. In 2013, over $178 billion (yes, billion with a B!) in retail sales was distributed through this model (an 8.1 percent increase from 2012) through more than 96 million independent distributors.[7]

This is all accomplished using the most effective and trusted form of advertising—word of mouth. Modern marketing is shifting away from traditional advertising to word of mouth advertising. As consumers in the 21st century, we trust recommendations from other people more than any other type of content.

---

7    www.wfdsa.org/files/pdf/global-stats/Sales_Report_2013.pdf

## Nielson Global Trust in Advertising Survey

| To what extent do you trust the following forms of advertising? | | |
|---|---|---|
| Global Average | Trust Completely/ Somewhat | Don't Trust Much/ At All |
| Recommendations from people I know | 92% | 8% |
| Consumer opinions posted online | 70% | 30% |
| Editorial content such as newspaper articles | 58% | 42% |
| Branded Websites | 58% | 42% |
| Emails I signed up for | 50% | 50% |
| Ads on TV | 47% | 53% |
| Brand sponsorships | 47% | 53% |
| Ads in magazines | 47% | 53% |
| Billboards and other outdoor advertising | 47% | 53% |
| Ads in newspapers | 46% | 54% |
| Ads on radio | 42% | 58% |
| Ads before movies | 41% | 59% |
| TV program product placements | 40% | 60% |
| Ads served in search engine results | 40% | 60% |
| Online video ads | 36% | 64% |
| Ads on social networks | 36% | 64% |
| Online banner ads | 33% | 67% |
| Display ads on mobile devices | 33% | 67% |
| Text ads on mobile phones | 29% | 71% |

Source: Nielsen Global Trust in Advertising Survey, Q3 2011

The more I learned about the business model, the more it made sense to me as a way for a company to move products into the marketplace in an effective way. Every company invests in marketing their product to the marketplace. The reallocation of funds from traditional marketing into word of mouth, referral-based marketing is quickly becoming a growing trend for companies. Instead of spending millions of dollars on TV advertisements, brand endorsement, etc., companies are creating great traction in the marketplace for their products and services operating via the network marketing business model.

For you and me, this is a very good thing, as it gives us all the opportunity to create a business distributing established products and services, without a lot of the risk associated with launching a business the traditional way. Since the model is based on actual performance in the marketplace, I finally had the ability to produce more for the company, and earn more compensation—unlimited compensation, really. Until this point, I had often felt overworked and underpaid, like countless others in our society. This model is built on leverage and teamwork. You are able to build a team of individuals all representing the bigger brand, and earn override commissions [commissions based on the sales of others] on your organization's performance. Instead of earning based on 100 percent of your own efforts, you are able to earn a percentage on the efforts of your team as well. I would always rather earn 1 percent on the efforts of 100, compared to 100 percent on my own efforts. That leverage is what makes network marketing such a brilliant way to earn a passive, residual income.

Network marketing is a lifestyle-friendly business in which you can work part-time outside of your full-time occupation, creating a secondary, Plan B income. It does not require you to quit your day job; it is best to start part-time! What many people do not realize is that most of us engage in network marketing every single day, we are just never paid for it. Network marketing is simply recommending and promoting a product or service you use and enjoy the benefits of, which is something we already do on a daily basis. We are always recommending products and services we enjoy—such as restaurants, websites, hairdressers, movies, and many more—without the expectation of compensation. Network marketing companies simply invest their marketing dollars differently, compensate their members for their recommendation, and even allow them to build their own distribution team and earn an income off of their efforts as well.

| PLAN A | TRADITIONAL EMPLOYMENT | PLAN B | NETWORK MARKETING |
|---|---|---|---|
| 40 Hours a Week | | 20 Hours a Week | |
| 50 Weeks a Year | | 50 Weeks a Year | |
| 40 Years | | 4 Years | |
| 80,000 hours of cumulative work | | 4,000 hours of cumulative work | |

Conceptual Credit: Jordan Adler, Author of *Beach Money*

Starting your own network marketing business is financially the most cost-effective business you can start. The Ewing Marion Kauffman Foundation estimated in 2009 that the average cost to start your own business was just over $30,000. The majority of franchises run anywhere from $50,000 to $200,000 to get started.[8] Most people do not have that kind of extra money kicking around and have to borrow money in order to start a business, putting them behind the debt eight ball from day one. Considering the typical new business in the United States is no longer in operation five years after being founded[9], the risk/reward is often enough to paralyze people with fear over the risk involved, and they never make the shift from being an employee to a business owner. Network marketing allows everyone the ability to start their own business at a much lower initial financial

---

8     www.franchising.com/howtofranchiseguide/the_cost_of_opening_a_franchise.html
9     http://smallbiztrends.com/2012/12/start-up-failure-rates-the-definitive-numbers.html#comments

investment, often only a few hundred dollars. Don't get me wrong—many network marketing businesses fail as well, but the loss is usually minimal in comparison. Unlike my personal training career, I didn't need any particular education or background to develop a successful business. Network marketing does not require a higher education to become successful. In fact, if you look at many great entrepreneurs, such as Bill Gates, Steve Jobs, Mark Cuban, Richard Branson (and the list goes on), many of them never received a post-secondary education. I spent much more on my post-secondary education than I have spent on my network marketing business, and the outcomes from each are not even comparable.

I fell in love with the ability to not only advance my own financial future, but to empower others as well. As an employee in the traditional workplace, you are always trying to work your way up the corporate ladder into a better position, only to find out that your ladder is leaning up against the wrong wall. A raise can often lead to more income, but also requires more hours, which is the one commodity we want to have more of in the end. Usually, our success is not based on empowering others, but making ourselves look better and more valuable compared to our co-workers. Network marketing flips the game, and allows you to empower others around you to succeed, because when your people win, you win. Our model truly exemplifies the Zig Ziglar quote "If you help enough people get what they want, you'll get everything you want." The most successful people in our profession are those who are the most effective at bringing out the greatest from within people and helping their team succeed. To make it an even more beautiful model, the only way you are ever compensated is when high quality products and services wind up in the end user's hands, bettering the individual's life. You make money when you help people, which to me feels like the best business in the world.

This wealth building profession is endorsed by countless business professionals in the world today, including Robert Kiyosaki, Donald Trump, Mark Victor Hansen, Paul Zane Pilzer, Bob Proctor, David Bach, and even "the greatest investor in the world," Warren Buffett. It is completely legal, with governments even offering tax benefits to those operating a network marketing business. The average tax savings range from $3,500 to $7,000, with some people in the higher tax brackets saving more than $12,000 per year.[10] Anyone who is solely an employee and has no home-based business is paying too much in taxes. The tax savings alone from engaging in the network marketing business model are substantial. I encourage you to talk to a local tax professional about how you can take advantage of the benefits a home-based business will offer you this tax season.

Maybe you will take an extra vacation with your tax savings! Most of us are allocated two weeks of vacation time per year from our employers and don't earn anything during this time except for maybe some vacation pay. Wouldn't it be nice if you continued to earn a consistent income even while you are on vacation, attending your child's sporting events, or sleeping? Network marketing offers this to us. Since we are paid on the value our organization brings to the company and not just on our own individual efforts, the work we are doing today will continue to provide for our future as long as value is still being provided to the company. There are people I introduced my products to more than five years

10    www.lmsuccess.com/Tax_Savings.html

ago who have consistently ordered monthly ever since, and I have earned an income passively from those purchases.

I truly experienced the marvel of residual income in June of 2014 when I married my wife, Vanessa. Most young couples struggle to pay for their wedding, not to mention their honeymoon (which often gets delayed or financed). After their big day, they race off to their jobs, away from each other, for 40-plus hours a week to pay off their bills and their wedding. I was able to take the entire month of June off from my business, get married, take a two-week honeymoon to Hawaii, and have it all paid for from my network marketing commissions that month. In fact, that was my highest earning month ever to that point, and I was on a beach with my new bride for most of the month! This luxury was a result of the business we had been building full time for the past two-and-a-half years. I went to college for two years, worked at my job for almost three years, and none of those ever paid me a cent unless I was there, trading my time for money. I worked three years as a full-time trainer, but I have not earned a paycheck since the day I quit, because I obviously no longer show up for work. By building a network marketing business, you are able to create a type of time and financial freedom not possible through traditional employment—a true residual income.

Your business is also a will-able asset, a true legacy business. If something were to happen to me as an employee, my only real hope for providing for my loved ones would be through life insurance or whatever savings I had been able to accrue. Now we have the benefit of the asset our network marketing business is to us, and future generations will continue to earn commissions on our business. This asset not only can be willed to your loved ones, but it can be bought and sold like any other business as well. When you take the time to build a network marketing business, you are not only working on creating a better financial future for yourself, but also for the next generation as well!

Everything I had been looking for in my "dream business" I found in network marketing: Unlimited earning potential, flexible, low start-up cost, no education required, tax advantages, and income that is residual and will-able. For me, and millions of others, this is the business model of our dreams and an opportunity of a lifetime to escape our current life sentence, and experience true freedom.

# CHAPTER
# FIVE

*Can I Escape?*

In short, yes. I may have accomplished quite a successful feat, but I was not any better equipped to accomplish this task than you are. Success is not guaranteed in network marketing any more than success is guaranteed in other professions. Most people quit before they ever have a chance to see success, and the only way to ensure failure is to quit. I wasn't willing to quit, although I felt like doing so many times, but I was committed to the process of building my own four-year career as a network marketing professional. I had a burning desire to succeed, a commitment to work, and a willingness to be mentored. And, most of all, I had a burning desire for my life to have true purpose and meaning.

Growing up, I was very undersized for my age. I felt like I didn't fit in with others around me, especially the other males (maybe because I grew up in rural Canada and never played hockey like the rest of my friends). I lacked self-confidence and self-esteem, and struggled with depression, which led to alcoholism in college. At one point, I even made the decision that I didn't belong, and that if I weren't around it wouldn't matter to anybody. I felt I wasn't worthy of achieving success. I was lost, without purpose and direction. It is surreal to think this was the place I was in four short years ago.

Gratitude is one of the most powerful emotions a human can experience, and without gratitude, success can be in vain. I believe God put network marketing in my life to pull me out of a downward spiral and lead me to a life of serving others. For that, I am grateful. Before network marketing, I couldn't even lead myself effectively, and now I have the privilege and honor of currently leading more than 35,000 business partners, not to mention the countless others I have met and inspired over the past few years. This business model has transformed every facet of my life, and I want that and more for everyone reading these words today. One of the best leadership and personal development programs on the planet is our business model.

Change is never easy, but it is worth it. Four years ago, I found myself at a crossroads in my life, as I made the shift from being a traditional employee to becoming a network marketing professional. I would be lying if I said the transition was easy, but as you can see, it was worthwhile. I was able to make a shift in my thinking and actions four years ago, generating different results in my life, and assisting thousands of others to do the same. Remember, insanity is doing the same thing over and over again, and expecting a different outcome. We are caught in a paradigm that is not designed to be broken out of or changed, but conformed to. This won't be the easiest journey—the path to becoming a self-employed business owner by becoming a network marketing professional—but it will be worth it. Most people wouldn't consider getting a degree to be an easy journey, yet hundreds of thousands embark in that direction every year, a road well-worn and financed. The beauty of this business is it complements what you already do, working full-time on your job and part-time on your fortune, much like I did. In the end, the choice is up to you to make.

If I were reading this book four years ago, I'd have found every point possible to disconnect myself from the author, looking for all the excuses in the world for why this wasn't for me, how I couldn't succeed at everything laid out before me, that this must just be "too good to be true." I was a master of making excuses. Fortunately, I have matured beyond that point. I realized I could either make excuses or I could make more money, but I couldn't make both. Now, instead of trying to find reasons why it wouldn't/couldn't work for me, I direct that same amount of energy and effort I previously would have put toward making excuses, toward a productive way of finding ways to make it possible and realistic for me. You have those same choices laid out in front of you right now.

I am no super human wonder boy. I am an average human with above average goals and aspirations, who committed to a process of personal and professional development to a new business and skill set and put in my due diligence and time. Believe me, if I can achieve this, you can as well. Everyone has a unique past, something that no one else has experienced but you. Be grateful for your past, the lessons you have learned have brought you to your present day self. You can't change the past, but you can make the most of your future. As you take steps towards creating the life you deserve, keep a grateful heart and mind, through the good times and the bad. I can promise you, the journey to your best life is not one that will always be easy, but it will be worth it. Commit to yourself today, going forward, that you will take every single thing life throws at you, be grateful for the experience, find the good in it, and move forward. Although there are things in my past that are apparent lowlights for me, I know I would not be where I am today without those "negative" experiences. Embrace your past, prepare for your future! I believe in you, and look forward to reading your success story of breaking out and doing something magnificent with your life!

# NOW THAT YOU HAVE READ THIS BOOK

This opportunity is not for everyone, and it is just that—an opportunity. It is not a game or the lottery. You can earn a few hundred, or a few thousand, or a lot more every month. The sky is not the limit in this case—you are! Our success depends on our enthusiasm for what we do, our commitment, and our skills. We will teach you everything we know, and the rest is up to you. The reason somebody gave you this book is because they are building their own asset income in a company for which they have a huge passion. They love the products, and they are inspired by the people with whom they are partnered. What they are trusting by giving you this is that it will inspire you to at least take a look. If you are willing, let them know. I know they are excited to show it to you. Please contact the person who gave you this book, and let them know you are willing to at least take a look. Your future awaits you!

# ACKNOWLEDGEMENTS

It would be foolish to think I could have grown my business alone. I have had a lot of help and support along the way from those closest to me. This book is a small dedication to those who I have leaned on for wisdom and support over the past few years.

My parents Bill and Carla Green have always supported me in all my endeavors and provided a household that allowed me to grow into the individual I am today.

Through my business I met my beautiful wife, Vanessa, who keeps me grounded and humble, always striving to become better and to put the most important things in life first—God and family. I love you more every day as we get to travel the world and change lives together.

My story would not be possible without an amazing team by my side. I am grateful for all members of our Green Team that work hard every day to create a world filled with wellness, purpose, and abundance. Thank you to all our leaders for trusting me to lead you!

This book might not have happened without the mentoring Richard Bliss Brooke provided me. No one encouraged me more to make this dream a reality, as he provided connections, allocated resources, and believed in me even when I didn't believe in myself.

I have had so many other mentors who have poured countless hours of coaching into me, allowing me to accomplish so much at a young age. There are too many people in this category to list, and I am honored to pay it forward in mentoring the next generation of networkers. So many saw greatness inside of me before I ever thought it existed, and I am forever grateful for the investment so many have made in my life.

Lastly, I have to give all the credit and glory to God, the creator of all things. Amazing love, grace, and guidance is available to all those who seek it through You. There is much more to this life than earning a paycheck and collecting material possessions. Through the abundance we have been given, continue to provide guidance to us on how we can bless others and speak life into those around us.

# RECOMMENDED RESOURCES TO ASSIST YOUR JAILBREAK

*The Four Year Career*
Richard Bliss Brooke

*GoPro: 7 Steps to Becoming a
Network Marketing Professional*
Eric Worre

*Building an Empire*
Brian Carruthers

*Beach Money*
Jordan Adler

*Rock Your Network Marketing Business*
Sarah Robbins

Rise of the Entrepreneur Documentary

# ABOUT THE AUTHOR

In a short four years, Adam Green has gone from a personal trainer earning $30,000 annually to a self-employed entrepreneur earning a seven-figure residual income, having found his success through the wealth building profession of network marketing. By the age of 25, Adam had developed an organization spanning more than 30 countries and producing millions in monthly sales volume while positively impacting countless families. His success has been documented in publications such as Networking Times Magazine, Success From Home Magazine, and the best-selling book *"The Four Year Career."* The pinnacle of Adam's financial success was reached August 14th, 2014 when, at the age of 25, he paid off his mortgage in full, 20 years ahead of the amortization schedule, officially becoming debt free. Today, Adam is living a life of purpose, empowering others to succeed and accomplish their dreams. Through his business, Adam met his beautiful wife Vanessa. They live in Red Deer, Alberta, Canada, when they are not traveling the world together.

# CONNECT WITH ADAM GREEN!

**f**    www.facebook.com/OfficialAdamGreen

**O**    www.instagram.com/AdamGreenYL

**y**    www.twitter.com/AdamGreenYL

**in**    www.linkedin.com/in/AdamGreenYL

**O**    @Adam_Green

www.25ToLifeBook.com

#25ToLifeBook